LISA COMFORT

SEW OVER IT

SEW IT, WEAR IT, LOVE IT

EBURY
PRESS

CONTENTS

INTRODUCING
MYSELF

Sewing has been in my life since I was a little girl. My earliest sewing memory is making a cross stitch placemat, aged six, only to find that I had sewn it to my skirt. I had to cut through all my work and start again.

I grew up in a beautiful village in North Yorkshire. The only downside was that, at the local primary school, I was the only girl in my year. But this turned out to be a blessing in disguise… I wasn't interested in football and making dens, so needles and thread became my best friends.

My parents and sister were never interested in crafts. Instead it was our childminder, Mrs Robinson, who introduced me to sewing. Every day after school we would sew drawstring bags and embroider them while my elder sister played out with her friends.

For my 11th birthday, my parents bought me a second-hand sewing machine. It was the best present I had ever received. Mrs Robinson showed me the basics and I made up the rest. Some interesting skirts, trousers and dresses followed, of which most were disasters, but I carried on. I couldn't wait to study textiles at school and it was in this class that I got my first sewing injury. I was furiously finishing my final project – a patchwork quilt – when I inadvertently let my finger slip under the needle and stitched straight through my finger. All I could think was, 'Oh no! I have ruined my work,' then came the throbbing pain. As my teacher rushed me to the school nurse, she whispered, 'You're a real seamstress now, Lisa.' That made my year.

I deviated from the sewing path and studied French and Italian at uni. In Italy, on my year abroad, I struck lucky and found an amazing dressmaking and pattern-cutting course and spent my days learning the fine art of sewing instead of studying Italian, as I should have been. Italians really know how to sew, especially Giulietta, a true master. She taught us how to sew buttonholes by hand (forcing us to start from scratch if they were anything but perfect) and how to tailor jackets so they fitted like a glove. I was in heaven. I sometimes still catch myself annotating my patterns in Italian: *orlo, vita, fianchi*…. Soon after, I realised languages weren't my true calling and that dressmaking was.

I love being able to make my own clothes, knowing that no one will have the same dress. You know when you go shopping and often there is something that is not quite right, when you make your own clothes, you can make everything right, exactly how you want it. It also means you can afford clothes made out of beautiful fabrics that otherwise would be out of your reach. Fabric shopping gives me a bigger buzz than clothes shopping and I feel less guilty as I know I am going to get so much for my money. At home I have an overflowing box, full of gorgeous silks, wools and cottons waiting to be brought to life. It is definitely my vice!

I START SEWING FOR A LIVING…

When I graduated, I moved to London, eager to find work and start earning money. I got an office job in the city and as soon as I had paid off some of my student debt, I decided to pursue

a career in what I really loved. A year of working life had showed me how tiresome it can be if you don't enjoy what you do. I believe in the philosophy that if you don't like it, then change it. So I did! I secretly applied to the London College of Fashion, only telling people when I got in. Halfway through the first year I was introduced to Bruce Oldfield, who not only gave me work experience while I was studying, but offered to be my mentor. After a year of college I left to work full time for Bruce. Giving up was not something I was used to, but I've no regrets because for me, picking up the tricks of the trade from his seamstresses and absorbing all I could from his pattern cutters outweighed another year of uni. It was while I was there that I gave myself the ultimate sewing challenge – to make a wedding dress for my cousin. It was a duchess satin gown, with hand appliquéd French lace, an internal corset and an embroidered veil. It took me over a hundred hours of blood (lots of pin pricks), sweat and tears but it was my proudest sewing achievement… and my cousin looked stunning.

From Bruce's I went on to work for Philippa Lepley, a bridal couture designer, as her fittings manager. By now I had been involved in the fashion world for almost three years but surprisingly I still wasn't content. I had a niggle and it was here that I felt the first stirrings of the need to go it alone. I wasn't sure how, I just knew that I wanted my own business.

…AND THEN I START TO TEACH

I had started to teach sewing privately at the weekends while working at Bruce's, tramping around London with my machine. Slowly, the number of customers grew and I realised how much I was enjoying teaching. Was this the idea I was waiting for? I was passionate about it and had already started to earn money, so I had a gut feeling that it would be a success. I bit the bullet and quit my job and moved to a bigger flat where I could run classes from my living room. I built it up bit by bit, slowly but surely.

I knew from the start what I wanted to achieve with Sew Over It: to spread the sewing word and show people how practical, creative and therapeutic it can be. I really believe that sewing can soothe the soul. It seems that sewing has skipped a generation and if young people don't learn the skill, it will die with our grandparents. I guess it happened in the sixties, when clothes became cheaper and people didn't need to make their own clothes, they could afford items on the high street. Nowadays the high street has almost outdone itself, providing affordable fashion, but nothing is unique. This is the draw to vintage clothes – there's nothing like a one-off. Dressmaking gives you the same buzz. You know that when you walk into a party or a wedding, your dress will be the only one. So I had the why, I just needed to solve the how…

SEW OVER IT IS BORN

For the start-up fund I scrimped and saved every penny and was fortunate to have help from a family member. Then came the six-month search for the property. When I found it, I knew it was right. I wanted to create a homely

THE
CUSTOMISING
TREE

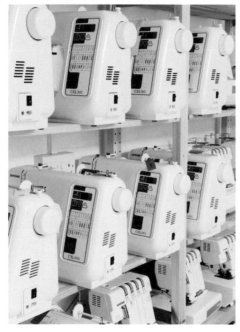

space where you would want to spend an afternoon learning to sew and meeting others who shared the passion. I filled it with all my favourite things and built a sewing haven in Clapham, South London.

Downstairs is where we run the classes. At the time of writing, there are 30 different classes from an introduction to sewing to making dresses based on the TV series *Madmen*; from soft furnishings and customising clothes and making leather bags. I like to have variety of choice and, most importantly, include projects that were chic and stylish. The fifties and sixties are my favourite eras and they will always feature heavily in my dressmaking classes (hence the Madmen dresses!).

Upstairs is the sewing café and shop where people drop in and pay per hour to use the machines and space. The shop is full of sewing trinkets and treasures and beautiful fabrics. The Sew Over It team is made up of some wonderfully creative ladies, all of whom share my passion for sewing. They help keep Sew Over It exciting and inviting. Sandro, our wonderful baker, provides the best cakes in London. I have a very big sweet tooth and am addicted to tea, so they had to be part of the plan!

Fortunately my idea was well received and I am so thankful to all the customers who have supported us in our first months and who keep coming back to our classes. It is thanks to them that I have been blessed with the best business I could have dreamed of. A day in the life of Sew Over It can see me teaching, designing new creations for classes, advising customers on their projects and that's just at the shop. Sew Over It takes me to other

The chalkboard in the image reads:

OUR CLASSES

Intro to sewing
Button me cushion
Men survival class

Fabric jewellery
Leather bag
Make up bag
Knitting club
Chillax knitting
Chillax crochet
Christmas classes

Intro to dressmaking
Pencil skirt
Ultimate wrap dress
Pussy bow blouse
Ultimate shift
Party dress
Chic cape

places too. We run children's sewing parties all over London, we host office sewing lunchtime sessions and I have just started running sewing breaks for Cath Kidston in a beautiful spa hotel in Cornwall. Sew Over It is more exciting than I ever dreamed it would be.

As the business goes from strength to strength there are more and more avenues to be explored. I have many hopes and ideas for the future of Sew Over It (although I am reluctant to write them down in case I jinx them). Currently, we are planning our online shop, which will sell fabrics from all over the world as well as our own Sew Over It merchandise range.

THIS IS THE *SEW OVER IT* BOOK

Writing this book has been the perfect end to the most exciting year of my life. It means that I can spread the sewing word a little further than my café and offer a slice of Sew Over It to those of you who aren't close by. I have added the ingredients into this book that I have in my café: a variety of ideas, inspiration and projects that are both practical and stylish. I hope that there is something in it for everyone.

Even if you have never picked up a needle and thread, you will be able to follow the projects. The book concentrates on what my current customers are most interested in learning: customising and altering, as well as making some creative projects from scratch. The best way to start is by making simple changes to your existing clothes. You can then see how very little effort can make a big difference. Customising is also a great money saver as it can save items from the charity

pile. Fabric scraps and buttons don't cost very much, but can make clothes look more chic instantly.

I couldn't write a sewing book without a chapter on altering clothes – the most practical of skills to have. There are a lot of tips on making things smaller, but I'd like to point out that this isn't a book for skinny people, it's just that making clothes bigger is much trickier! I will have to include that in a future book. I have also included some of my favourite accessories – they will jazz up any outfit. And finally I wanted to give you something to aspire to – dressmaking from scratch in the 'Challenge Yourself' chapter.

I hope that you will enjoy making these projects and feel free to put your own twist on them. But, most importantly, I hope that – as it is to me – sewing will become a friend of yours too.

INTRODUCING
THE NEEDLE AND THREAD

CHOOSE A NEEDLE

Needles come in different lengths and sizes. Some people prefer using a long needle and others a short one. Try them out and decide which you prefer. The width of the needle required is determined by the task. If you are taking up a hem or making slip stitches (see page 25), you will need a fine needle. If you are hand-stitching heavy fabric, you will need a thicker needle.

THREAD

It seems fussy, but there are good threads and bad threads. For sewing by hand and machine, 100 per cent polyester is better. It is stronger and finer and tends not to knot as easily. You can buy poor-quality and good-quality thread and your machine may be very sensitive to this – mine is. But even for hand-stitching it is worth buying the best you can, as you will find it doesn't snap easily or tangle. To test the quality, snap the thread – if it breaks really easily, then this means it's poor quality. The stronger the thread the better.

THREAD A NEEDLE AND OFF YOU GO

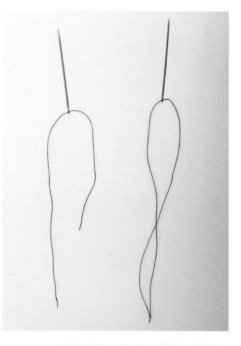

In this book you will be using either a single or double thread. With a single thread, you can adjust the length of the thread as you sew. With a double thread, you thread through the needle and double up the thread by tying the two ends together.

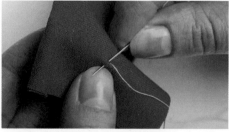

SECURE STITCH

When starting any hand-sewn stitch I always tie a knot in the end of the thread. I also make a little backstitch into the fabric (see opposite) to anchor my thread securely before I start sewing. A knot is never enough.

MAGIC KNOT

When you finish a hand-sewn stitch it is a good idea to make both a backstitch and a magic knot, which sits flush against the fabric. Tie a knot in the thread, close to the fabric, then use the needle to push the knot down, allowing the knot to tighten at the same time. This way you will get the knot sitting flat against the fabric.

STITCHES

TACKING

A long running stitch that is temporarily holding something in place. You can also tack using a sewing machine.

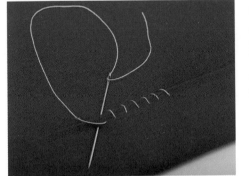

OVERSTITCH

Just as it says – use this stitch when you stitch over an edge or fold. You can use it along the fabric edge or work it over and over in the same spot for strength.

BACKSTITCH

Like a running stitch but stronger. I use one backstitch to anchor my thread, but it can also be used in place of a machine-made stitch. If small, it can be strong.

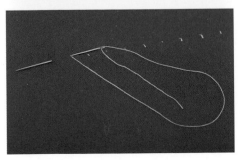

SLIP STITCH

A great little discreet stitch. One of my students once called it the stealth stitch – it's undercover! It is a stitch for sewing folded edges, especially when hemming a garment. Alternate between running the needle inside the fold and then picking up a thread or two from the main fabric.

INTRODUCING THE SEWING MACHINE

Here are some of my top tips for using a sewing machine. I have to say that I think you will get on much quicker with your machine if you go to a class as there are some basics that are much better learnt in person. You will also find that you have the confidence to do more if you have been shown the foundations.

✂ If your machine is not stitching properly, nine times out of ten it is due to the threading. Even if you think you haven't made a mistake, re-thread it from scratch.

✂ Always remember to put the presser foot down before you begin to stitch. This is one of the most common mistakes in our classes.

✂ Use 100 per cent polyester thread. Your machine will thank you and will behave better.

✂ Don't forget to thread through the thread take-up, or the rabbit, as I like to call it as I think this part of the machine looks like a rabbit with a floppy ear and an eye! Often the thread doesn't get caught properly through the eye of the rabbit and when this happens the machine goes haywire.

✂ Always reverse at the start and end of every seam. Starting at the edge of the fabric, sew three stitches forward, then three stitches backwards and then continue down the rest of the seam. Repeat at the end.

✂ Thread your machine with a thread that matches the fabric. When choosing your thread colour, unravel a bit and place the strand of thread against the fabric – this will give you a better idea rather than holding the reel up to it. If you can't get a perfect match, then it is always best to go darker on dark fabrics and lighter on pale, pastel fabrics.

✂ Don't cut your thread too short from the needle. If you do, the needle will keep unthreading. Keep 10–15 cm (4–6 in) of thread out of the needle.

✂ It is always a good idea to have a little practice before you start a project. Use an off-cut of the fabric you will be sewing and practise a couple of seams. This is particularly important when using an unusual fabric such as tulle. It will help you work out the best way to hold and guide the fabric and what speed you are most comfortable sewing at. Remember the trickier the fabric, the slower you should be sewing.

CUSTOMISING
CLOTHES

TAKE STOCK OF YOUR CLOTHES

Customising is about looking at what you already have and making it feel new again. I dedicate an evening every couple of months for just me and my wardrobe where I look at everything I have and have a good sort out. I play dress-up, sifting through every item in my wardrobe and asking myself what can I do to change this. These are the steps to follow:

✂ Organise your wardrobe into categories, such as skirts, dresses and trousers. In that way you can see what you actually have. If you're really sad like me, you can always colour code them – just for fun, of course!

✂ Everyone has clothes that they absolutely love and are perfect – you don't need to worry about those so put them to one side – I always say, 'If it ain't broke, don't fix it!'.

✂ With the rest of your clothes, try them on and decide why you don't like them. Is it because they don't fit you? Or is it because they are boring? Or because the colour doesn't suit you? Ask yourself such questions as: 'What if I made this shorter, would I like it then?', 'What if I changed these buttons?'.

✂ Try out different combos. Add items with other items, try out layering, get your accessories and belts involved – they can make a difference. I always notice what others are wearing as they may have better ideas of how to put clothes together. Keep your eyes open when you're out and about and take mental notes of outfits that you like.

✂ Hopefully, after some effort you will have already saved some items from rejection by just putting them together differently.

✂ For those that are left, divide them into the 'Don't fit me', 'Boring' and 'The why did I buy these?' piles. Some may be beyond saving, but hopefully a few can be made more exciting and interesting after applying some of the ideas in this chapter.

SEW ON A BUTTON

Buttons became my new best friends a few years back when I realised I could transform a dull cardie into a chic little number by simply swapping the buttons. They are one of the easiest and most effective ways of customising your clothes.

It may seem pretty basic, but a lot of people out there don't know how to sew on a button. If sewn badly, they will just keep falling off, which will drive you potty. Here are the essential steps.

YOU WILL NEED
Pins
Needle
Thread
Button(s)
Scissors

1   If you are replacing buttons, make sure you sew the new ones in exactly the same place. If you are adding buttons for the first time, don't be afraid to get out the tape measure and mark their positions properly. The easiest way to do this is to make a cross with two pins. Where they cross will be the centre of the button once it is stitched in place.

2   Take a double thread and tie a knot in the end. Starting from the inside, push the needle to the outside and make a little secure stitch.

3   Pass the needle up through one of the holes in the button and back down another. For a two-hole button it's easy, just pass the needle up through one hole and down through the other. And for a button with a shaft (a bit that sticks out underneath), just thread the needle in and out of the hole.

4 If it is a four-hole button, you can either stitch diagonally, creating a cross, alternating between each pair of holes, or you can stitch two parallel lines, again alternating through the holes.

5 For a shirt or cardie, stitch four to five times through each hole and for a coat, six to seven times, so it's extra strong.

6 Finishing with the needle on the inside, thread the needle up through the fabric but not through the button. Wrap the thread round itself three or four times, covering the stitches. This is a little protective layer of thread that stops the stitches getting worn down.

7 Then it's back to the inside again with that needle. Make another little secure stitch and a magic knot (see page 24) to finish off. Cut off the thread. Now that button ain't going anywhere!

▲ Adding buttons to the shoulder seams can give clothes a military look.

◀ Replacing a boring black cardie's buttons with pearl or gold ones brings instant hints of Chanel.

◀▲ Use buttons to highlight a waistline or a neckline.

MAKE SELF-COVERED BUTTONS

I recently became addicted to these little treasures. They come in different sizes and are so simple to cover. Once you know how to make them, you will be putting them everywhere, trust me. They work best with lightweight cotton, such as cotton lawn. Steer clear of heavier fabrics as they can be too thick. When it comes to choosing colours and patterns, you are the designer, so whatever you say goes! As a guide, plain fabrics stand out more, pattern fabrics add more texture.

YOU WILL NEED
Self-covering button(s) (two parts)
Fabric
Pencil
Scissors
Needle
Thread
Pliers

1 There are two parts to a self-covering button: the front is curved with little teeth around the edge, and the back piece is flat with a ridge on one side.

2 Place the fabric wrong side up on your work surface and put the front piece of the button on to it. Draw a circle around the button, approximately 1 cm (½ in) larger than the button. Cut out the circle.

3 Take the needle and thread and sew a little running stitch about 2 mm (⅛ in) from the edge of the fabric. Don't tie a knot in the thread, but leave a tail of thread at the start and end instead. Keep your stitches quite small so they will gather up neatly.

4 Place the front of the button, curved side down in the middle of the fabric. Pull both tails of thread so the fabric gathers around the button. Pull the threads as tight as you can. Then push the fabric into the base of the button.

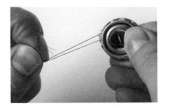

5 Holding the gathering in place (don't let go of the thread until the last moment), lay the button back, ridge side down, over the button front, slotting it over the metal loop. Then press down on a hard surface so that it clicks. You may need to use pliers as some self-covering buttons are a little stiff. Keep the pliers at the edge of the button otherwise you could dent it.

6 Cut off the thread and sew the button onto whatever you like.

▲ These buttons were covered with a pair of wool tights.

▲ I wanted to add colour to this cardie so I used a different fabric for each button.

SEW BEADS AND SEQUINS ONTO CLOTHES

This is my new favourite pastime. I guess it's the magpie in me, but I love sparkles and gems. I also find sewing them onto clothes really relaxing. Beading is the ultimate television-watching project.

I find it most effective if you mix up the types and shapes of beads. Sticking to one colour, but then choosing different tones will make it look textured. Or you can mix up all the colours and the beads for something with impact.

YOU WILL NEED
Pins
Tape measure
Needle
Thread
Beading needle (a very fine needle to pass through tiny beads)
Beads or sequins
Nylon thread (the finer the better)
Scissors

For sequins, try using a more matt finish rather than the really shiny ones. This will look more subtle and less like bling!

There are so many different types of beads and they vary in price. I have used glass, stone, metal and plastic, from seed beads (really tiny ones) and bugles (tubular-shaped beads) to large round and cube-shaped ones, as in these projects. They work well together.

With regards to what can be beaded, you can use anything except leather and seriously heavy-duty fabrics as you will find that beading needles aren't strong enough to stitch through these fabrics. If you are beading delicate fabrics, be careful not to use beads that are too heavy as these will alter the shape and hang of the garment as well as potentially damage the weight. It is a bit like pasta – Italians would never put a heavy sauce with a fine linguine.

There is so much you can do with beading. You can bead a particular part of a garment, such as the lapel, collar or waistband; you can create an area and bead it; or just add a scattering of beads – going from dense to light.

PREPARING YOUR GARMENT

✂ If you are beading an area that is already designed, such as a collar, you don't need to mark where you are going to attach the beading, you can just start.

✂ If you are creating an area to bead, such as a width around a neckline, you will need to mark out the border so that you keep your beading neat. Decide on where you would like your beading to go and mark the edge with a few pins.

✂ If it is a neckline, like in the example on page 47, mark the depth of the beading in a few places with some pins and use a tape measure to be accurate. Then take a needle and contrasting thread and stitch a basic tacking line, joining up the pins. Remove the pins and this will be the edge of the beading.

SEWING ON SEQUINS

1 Take a beading needle and single nylon thread, tie a knot in the end and make a backstitch to secure. Starting from the inside of the garment, push the needle up through the fabric.

2 Thread a sequin onto the needle and push it down the thread until it is sitting against the fabric.

3 Holding it in place with your thumb, thread the needle back down into the fabric at the edge of the sequin.

4 Push the needle back up again, this time coming up on the other side of the sequin and then back down again in the hole of the sequin. You can then move onto the next sequin. It is fine to keep using the same nylon thread as long as the distance to the next sequin isn't too far. Work logically through your design, starting at one end and finishing at the other. Try not to hop about too much otherwise you will waste thread and create a cobweb effect behind.

SEWING SEED BEADS AND BUGLES

1 Take a beading needle and single nylon thread, tie a knot in the end and make a backstitch to secure. Starting from the inside of the garment, push the needle up through the fabric.

2 You can thread up to three seed beads or two bugle beads on your needle at a time, if this works with your design. Don't do more than that as they can then come loose. Push the beads down the thread to the fabric and pull the thread taut. Make sure they start where the thread comes up from the fabric.

3 Put the tip of the needle against the last bead that was strung and push the needle back down into the fabric.

4 If you are adding more seed beads, push the needle back up through the fabric before the last bead and pass it through this bead a second time. You can then add the next set of beads. This will ensure there are no gaps between the beads so the line is continuous.

▲ All of these lovely beads make this top much more delicate so gently hand wash it, making sure you don't pull on any of the threads.

SEWING ON LARGE BEADS

1 Take an ordinary sewing needle (you only need the beading needle for sewing on sequins) and single nylon thread, tie a knot in the end and make a backstitch to secure. Starting from the inside of the garment, push the needle up through the fabric.

2 Thread the bead on the needle and slide it down to the fabric. Holding the bead in place, push the needle back down into the fabric, without leaving too much of a gap from the bead hole. The thread should be as invisible as possible. If the bead is heavy, stitch a further time through the bead to make it extra secure.

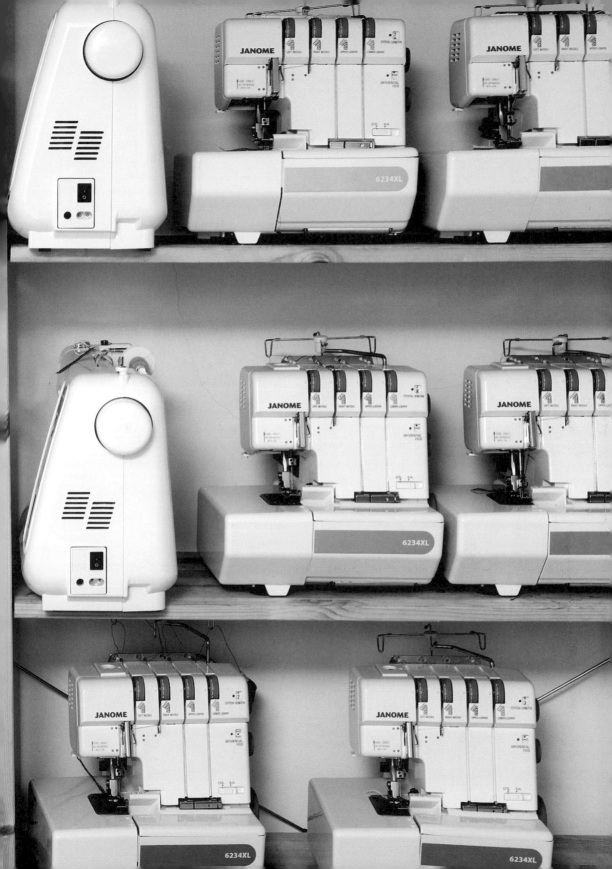

SEW MOTIFS ONTO CLOTHES

You see clothes with motifs in so many shops – they make clothes look more expensive, more interesting and perhaps more chic. But I bet you think they are tricky to sew. They're not! You will find a selection of motifs in a good haberdashery store or on eBay. They come in many varieties, from Venetian lace to beaded designs, from animals to letters. I tend to use them on cardies and tops, but there are no rules, so stitch them wherever you like.

You can stitch them on using a machine or by hand. Machine-stitching can be a little tricky, so if you are not confident, then hand-stitch them in place. For beaded motifs you will have to stitch by hand as the beads will break on the machine.

YOU WILL NEED
Fabric stabiliser (see page 52)
Scissors
Motif
Tape measure
Pins
Needle
Thread
Sewing machine with an embroidery
    foot

ATTACHING MOTIFS BY MACHINE

1   If you are going to be stitching a motif onto stretchy fabric like a T-shirt, you will need to back the shirt with fabric stabiliser. This is a fusible fabric that you iron onto the back of the garment where you will be stitching the motif. Cut a piece of stabiliser that is roughly the same size as the motif and lay it onto the reverse side of the fabric with the waxy/shiny side face down. Then iron it on, following the manufacturer's instructions. You can now attach the motif without worrying about the fabric distorting. If the fabric isn't stretchy but it is delicate, then it is a good idea to back it in this way, too.

2   Position the motif on your garment. If you are adding a pair, measure to make sure they are placed symmetrically. Use lots of pins to hold them in place as you sew.

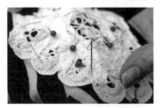

3   Tack the motif in place with a contrasting thread so it is easy to unpick. Ensure the stitches are secure – you don't want it moving when you start to sew it. Remove the pins.

4   On your sewing machine, change the presser foot to an embroidery foot and remove your feed dog (see opposite). Make sure the thread matches the colour of the motif as much as possible.

5   Change to a zigzag stitch and set the stitch length at 1 and the width at 1.5.

6   Stitch, following the edge of the motif. If it is lace, keep to the thicker areas of cording as the idea is to make the stitching as invisible as possible.

7   You will also need to stitch down some of the centre of the motif. If it is lace, stitch along the cording to the middle and then stitch back to the edge without stopping – it's a bit like drawing without taking your pen off the paper. If it is a solid motif, then just stitch into the middle as discreetly as possible.

8   Once the motif is stitched securely in place, cut off the threads.

9   Unpick the tacking thread and gently tear off the stabiliser at the back of the garment, taking care not to break the stitches. Don't worry if some little pieces stay, but tear off the majority.

TIPS FOR USING AN EMBROIDERY FOOT

✂ Not all machines have the option of removing the feed dog (little teeth), so check that yours does before buying an embroidery foot.

✂ Keep the fabric taut: if you don't, it can get pulled down into the machine.

✂ Keep the fabric moving: as the feed dog has gone there is nothing moving it through the machine – you have to do this.

ATTACHING MOTIFS BY HAND

1   For sewing on a motif by hand you
    probably won't need fabric stabiliser
    as the fabric won't be under so
    much strain. Just be careful not to
    stretch the fabric as you are sewing.
    Position, pin and tack the motif as
    in Steps 2 and 3 on page 52.

2   Take a needle and double thread.
    Following the outline of the motif,
    make very small overstitches (page
    25) wrapping them around the edge
    of the motif. If it is a lace motif, stitch
    over the cording, moving along
    underneath the motif. Finish with
    two small backstitches to secure.

3   You will also need to stitch along the
    middle of the motif to keep it firmly
    in place. Start at one end and stitch
    your way to the other end, as before,
    making your stitches as neat as
    possible. Finish off with a couple of
    small backstitches.

**WASHING GARMENTS WITH
ADDED MOTIFS**
Adding a motif will make your
garment more delicate and
therefore greater care is needed
when you wash it. If you have
hand-stitched a garment, then
always hand-wash it. If you have
used a sewing machine, you may
be able to wash it in a washing
machine, but use a gentle
programme.

ADD RIBBON TO YOUR CLOTHES

There are many ways of using ribbon to customise your clothes. You don't just have to tie bows – a ribbon can be funky, and not at all twee. Here are three ways of manipulating ribbon. I have taken four jumpers to show you how different they can look with a splash of ribbon.

YOU WILL NEED
Ribbon
Pins
Scissors
Shirring elastic (optional)
Needle
Thread
Sewing machine (optional)

FOLDED RIBBON

I think this works best around a neckline, but it can go anywhere. Use your ribbon to create abstract and asymmetrical patterns, folding it and pinning to the garment as you go.

1 Take any length, width or style of ribbon and fold it at random points.

2 At the folds, pin the ribbon to the garment and press in place. It may be easier to do this on the garment itself and is most effective when it looks uneven and irregular. Change the angle of the folds for more interesting patterns.

3 To attach the ribbon, take a needle and single thread, the same colour as the ribbon. Starting at one end, tuck under the cut edge of the ribbon and anchor it down in the middle of the ribbon with a couple of backstitches.

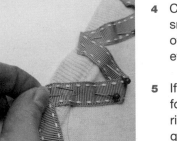

4 Continue stitching using either a very small running stitch along the middle of the ribbon or use a backstitch at every fold.

5 If you are using backstitch at each fold, move along underneath the ribbon and on the inside of the garment. This works best if the folds are close together.

6 Finish off in the same way you started, tucking the ribbon end under and anchoring with a couple of backstitches. Knot off on the inside and cut off the thread.

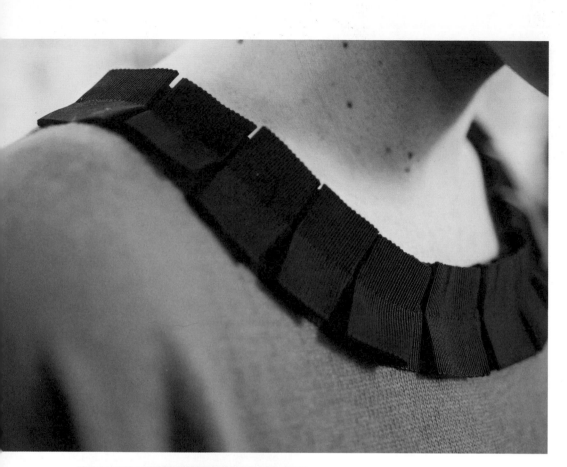

PLEATED RIBBON

If you are manipulating a pleated ribbon to go around curves, you may find it easier to stitch it on by hand. If you are stitching in straight lines, use a sewing machine. As a general rule, you will need three times the length of ribbon as the area you wish to cover – but, if in doubt, buy extra!

1   Use pins to mark where you are going to be folding the ribbon for pleats. Place four pins in the following positions for the first pleat:
    ■ Where you want the pleat to start
    ■ 2 cm (¾ in) along
    ■ Another 2 cm (¾ in) along
    ■ Another 3 cm (1¼ in) along, which marks the start of the next pleat. Repeat this for each pleat.

2   Fold the first pin to the second pin and then fold the third pin to the second pin in the opposite direction – so two pleats are meeting in the middle. Then there is a 3 cm (1¼ in) gap before the centre of the next pleat. Use the pins to hold the pleats in place and press for a sharper, flatter look.

3   Repeat Step 2 all along the ribbon until each pleat is pinned in place. Tack the pleats and remove the pins.

4   Pin the ribbon to the garment, placing the pins horizontally, which makes them easier to remove as you stitch.

5   To attach the ribbon with a machine, use a straight stitch to sew along the centre of the ribbon, reversing at the start and at the end to secure the seam. One row of stitching is enough to hold the ribbon in place.

6   For hand-stitching, stitch along the centre with a backstitch, securing it with a magic knot (see page 24) at either end.

ELASTICATED RIBBON

You can stitch elasticated ribbon in rows or you can twist it and create curved lines. It works best with double-sided ribbon, so that you can't tell if it is the front or back. If you are new to sewing by machine, you may find it easier to hand-stitch the ribbon, especially if you are creating twists and curves.

SHIRRING ELASTIC
You will be surprised how easy shirring elastic is to use. Just wind it on a bobbin and stitch as normal on your machine with a 100 per cent polyester thread for the top.

1   Thread your machine with shirring elastic (see below, left). Then set it to straight stitch with a stitch length of 2.5 and with the needle in the middle position. Stitch along the centre of the ribbon. Don't reverse at the start or end. The ribbon will gather up as you start to sew.

2   Leave tails of thread at either end – you can then pull the shirring elastic so it gathers further. Use either both of the top threads or both of the lower threads; it won't work if you are pulling the top thread and lower thread at same time.

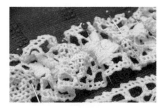

3   Pin the ribbon in place every 3 cm (1¼ in), pinning horizontally. Tuck the raw ends under so they are hidden. If your fabric is very stretchy, you may need to use some fabric stabiliser (see page 52).

4   To attach the ribbon with a machine, stitch over the elastic seam with a straight stitch, reversing at the start and end. You may need to pivot at some of the curves. To do this, lower your needle into the fabric and lift the presser foot so that you can negotiate the angle. Lower the presser foot again to continue.

5   For hand-stitching, sew down the middle of the ribbon with a backstitch, securing it with a knot at either end.

MAKE FABRIC BOWS

The old bow is hanging in there. We have seen centuries of bows and they are still being reinvented. Here's my twist on the subject.

Decide how much of a statement you want your bow to make. The choice of fabric changes the style. The addition of a bow or two is always going to be a girlie look, but black fabric makes it more elegant while floral keeps it feminine. Bear in mind, too, that the fabric needs to be lightweight as anything heavier like denim will be too stiff to tie and will stick out too much. Also think about placement – where will it go and what size bow will work best?

YOU WILL NEED
Strip of fabric (for amount, see Step 1)
Scissors
Pins
Ruler
Tailor's chalk (this is usually shaped as a flat triangle and can be used for drawing on fabrics. It comes in many colours)
Sewing machine
Thread
Needle

1   Take a strip of any fabric and tie a bow with it. Then roughly place it on the garment and adjust the size until you like the look. This will give you the approximate length and width required for the fabric. To make the bow in this photograph, I used a piece of fabric measuring 40 cm (15¾ in) long and 14 cm (5½ in) wide.

2   The bow will look better if the strip of fabric is cut on the bias. This means 45° from the selvedge (see page 110). The easiest way of finding the bias is to lay the fabric out flat. Take one corner and fold it over to the opposite diagonal corner, matching the edges. The fold line is the bias.

3   Iron the fold so there is an obvious crease, then use this as a starting point to mark out the fabric strip with the ruler and tailor's chalk. Cutting on the bias does mean you will need more fabric, so if you only have a small piece, then just cut a strip across or down the length of the fabric. It's not the end of the world not to have your fabric cut on the bias; it just makes it a bit easier if it is.

4 Fold the fabric strip for the bow in half lengthways, right sides together, matching the raw edges and pin all along the long edges. You may also want to iron the strip to help it stay in place.

5 Take the ruler and tailor's chalk and draw a diagonal line across both ends. Draw the line from the corner of the folded edge. This is your stitching line for the ends of the fabric strip.

6 Set your machine to straight stitch with a stitch length of 2.5 and with the needle in the middle position. Starting at the far point of one of the diagonal lines, stitch along the chalk line, reversing to secure.

7 When you get to 1 cm (½ in) before the long edge of the strip, stop, put the needle into the fabric, lift up the presser foot and pivot the strip so that it is aligned to sew down the long edge with a 1 cm (½ in) seam allowance. Drop the presser foot again and stitch all the way down, stopping when you reach the second chalk line. Reverse stitch to secure.

8 Cut off the loose threads and trim the fabric at both ends to 1 cm (½ in), matching the seam allowance of the long side. Turn the strip the right way round so the seam allowances are on the inside.

9 Place the strip on an ironing board with the seam to one side and press. At the open end, tuck the 1 cm (½ in) seam allowance into the strip. Press and pin in place.

10 Take a needle and single thread, tie a knot in the end and slip stitch the folded edges together. Backstitch and knot off at the end to secure. Now you can tie the strip into a bow.

11 To pin the bow correctly onto the garment it is best to do this when it is being worn, so borrow a friend or use a mannequin. Pin the ties of the bow and the loops securely in place and then ask your friend to carefully remove the garment or gently remove it from the mannequin.

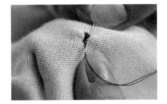

12 Take a needle and single thread to match the bow. How much you stitch it down is up to you, but you definitely need to stitch through the loops and ties and behind the knot. Use a slip stitch for the ties and loops. You will need to start afresh and knot off after each one. Don't carry your thread over to the next tie or loop – it is too far.

13 For the knot, turn the garment inside out and make three to four stitches through the middle to securely anchor it down. As these won't be visible don't be scared to make your stitches a little bigger.

14 Remove the pins. If you want to flatten your bow a little, then gently press it. If you are using delicate fabric, iron over a tea towel.

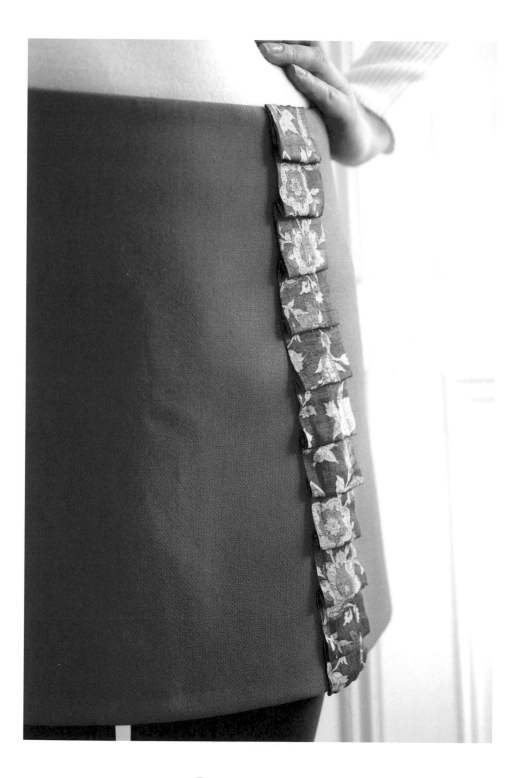

MAKE AND USE FABRIC STRIPS

This is a take on the pleated ribbon idea (see page 60). It works best if the strip matches the colour of the garment as it is then a subtler customising job, but you can, of course, use contrasting colours. Chiffon and georgette work beautifully, but you could also use a lightweight cotton or even satin for a more luxurious look.

YOU WILL NEED
Strip of fabric (for amount, see
    Steps 1 and 2)
Tape measure
Scissors
Pins
Sewing machine
Needle
Thread
Tailor's chalk
Ruler

1 Decide where the strip is going to go. You could add it down the length of a skirt or around the neckline. Play around with some fabric and see what works. Think about the width of the strip, too – you don't want it to take over the garment.

2 Cut out a piece of fabric running along or across the grain (see page 110) that measures:
   ■ Two times the desired width plus a 2 cm (¾ in) seam allowance
   ■ Three times the length of the area it is going to cover plus a 2 cm (¾ in) seam allowance.

3 Fold the strip in half lengthways, right sides together, matching the raw edges and pin. You may also want to iron the strip to help it stay in place.

4 Set your machine to straight stitch with a stitch length of 2.5 and with the needle in the middle position. Starting at one end, stitch along the long edge with a 1 cm (½ in) seam allowance. When you get to 1 cm (½ in) before the end of the strip, stop, put the needle into the fabric, lift up the presser foot and pivot the strip so that it is aligned to sew along the bottom with a 1 cm (½ in) seam allowance. Drop the presser foot again and stitch across the bottom. Trim the seam allowance to 5mm (¼ in) and turn the strip the right way round.

5 At the open end, tuck the 1 cm (½ in) seam allowance into the strip. Press and pin in place. Take a needle and single thread, tie a knot in the end and slip stitch the folded edges together. You will now have a tube of fabric with closed ends.

6 Place the tube on the ironing board with the seam in the middle of the underside and press so the edges are crisp.

7 Now for the pleating. Using a tape measure, put a pin every 2 cm (¾ in) along the length of the strip. You can, of course, change this measurement, but remember to allow for more fabric if your folds are going to be more frequent or larger.

8 Fold the first pin to the second pin, then fold the third pin to the fourth pin and so on. Each time use one of the pins to hold the pleat in place. Then take a needle and single thread and tack the pleats in place by stitching through the middle of the strip. Remove the pins.

9 Leave the pleats as they are for a soft finish or for a sharper, flatter look, press the folds.

10 To attach the strip to the garment, pin it in place, ideally on a mannequin or while being worn by a friend. Place the pins horizontally across the strip.

11 Either machine-stitch a single seam right through the middle of the strip or, if you prefer not to see any stitching, use a needle and thread and slip stitch around the edges.

PLAITED STRIPS

For an alternative take on this idea, you could plait your strips. This looks great around a neckline or cuffs, for example. You will need to make three strips and then have someone hold an end while you plait them together (see page 147). Pin both ends to secure the plait, then pin the plait to the garment and slip stitch along both sides of the plait, tucking under the ends to neaten.

ALTERING
CLOTHES

GENERAL TIPS FOR ALTERING CLOTHES

The best piece of advice I can give you when altering clothes is to ask a friend to help you. Pinning clothes on yourself is very fiddly and will usually result in frustration and inaccurate pinning. Here are a few other helpful tips:

✕ If you are making an alteration to both sides of a garment, rather than pinning both sides, just do one side and then transfer the information to the other side by measuring at various points.

✕ When deciding on a hem length, put on the shoes that you would wear with the outfit – heels can make a frumpy long hem look elegant and they can also make a shorter hem look cheap.

✕ Try it on before it's final. If you aren't 100 per cent sure about an alteration, try it on pinned first. Once you have cut and stitched, there's no turning back!

VINTAGE SHOPPING TOP TIPS

I find my vintage shopping trips are most fruitful when I am not looking for anything in particular. You have to be in the right mood for spending time rummaging – that's when you find the real treasures! Here are some points to consider when you are next on a vintage clothes hunt.

✂ Fit is the most important thing. If it's too small, put it back on the rail as it is much harder to make clothes bigger than it is to make them smaller. Choose something that fits you well on the bust area. If it is too big on the waist or too long, you can change that.

✂ Some of the best vintage dresses I have bought looked frumpy when I first tried them on, but when I lifted the hems, they suddenly became stylish. Shortening or lengthening a hem is not difficult, so don't discard clothes because of length.

✂ I often find that vintage dresses and tops have rather 'costumey' sleeves, usually far too billowy or too tight. If they are too big, there is lots you can do that I will show you in this chapter. If they are too tight, then it is a much trickier job, so best wait until you have built up your sewing skills.

✂ I am a stickler for finding stains. If the garment is stained, it is likely that it has been there a while and probably won't come out in the wash. So unless it can be covered with a motif, let it go, however fabulous it is.

✂ Often clothes in vintage shops can be quite creased. Don't let this put you off – try to see past the crumples!

TAKE UP HEMS: HOW TO PREPARE, MEASURE, PIN AND PRESS

If you love buying vintage clothes, then you will be familiar with the frustration of a perfect skirt or dress that is just too long. Shortening the hem can be the difference between something that is frumpy or funky. Once you know how, it's easy enough.

YOU WILL NEED
A friend (!)
Pins
Tape measure
Tailor's chalk
Scissors
Needle and thread
   (for a hand-stitched hem)
Sewing machine and thread
   (for a machine-stitched hem)
Ruler

TURNING UP A HEM

1 Try your skirt or dress on and ask a friend to pin up your garment to the desired length. Don't worry about making the hem even at this stage. All you actually need is one pin that marks the desired length.

2 Take off the skirt or dress and measure the difference from the pin to the existing hemline.

3 Take this measurement and subtract the amount needed for the hem. For a narrow hem, this is 1–2 cm (½–¾ in) and for a wide hem, over 2 cm (¾ in). The remaining figure is the amount that needs to be cut off.

4 Using the tape measure and tailor's chalk, mark this amount every 10 cm (4 in) or so around the hem. Remember to mark on the reverse of your skirt or dress. You will then be able to join the marks together with the tailor's chalk and ruler. This is your cutting line. Cut along the cutting line with scissors. Save your scraps for another project.

5 Fold over a little less than half of the hem width, 5 mm–1 cm (¼–½ in), depending on your choice of hem width, to the inside. Press with the iron. Then fold the remaining hem allowance and press with the iron.

6 Place some pins in the hem to hold it in place. Make sure the pins are facing the right direction, the head of the pin facing you and the point towards the machine – this makes them easier to remove as you sew.

SEWING A HEM BY HAND

1   You need good light for sewing
    a hem by hand and a fine needle.
    If your needle is too thick, you will
    struggle to do this accurately.

2   Take a needle and single thread. Tie
    a knot in the end and, starting at a
    side seam, make a little secure stitch
    to anchor your thread (see page 24).

3   You are now going to use hemming
    stitch to attach the turn-up of the
    hem to the skirt. Pick up two strands
    of fabric on the needle from the
    fabric next to the top of the turn-up.

4   Move along 5 mm (¼ in) and pass
    the needle through the folded edge
    from front to back. You can take
    more of a chunk of fabric on this
    side as it won't show.

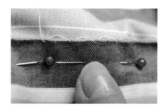

5   Move along another 5 mm (¼ in)
    and pick up two strands of fabric.
    You are stitching from side to side,
    moving along 5 mm (¼ in) after each
    stitch. Don't pull your stitches tightly
    as this will pucker the fabric.

6   Every 10 stitches or so, make a little
    secure stitch into the folded side.
    This will secure the stitches so that if
    you catch one and pull it, it will only
    pull out those 10 stitches.

7   One length of thread won't get you
    all the way round. Finish off and start
    again on the folded side so it doesn't
    show. Finish off by making a secure
    stitch and tying a knot.

8   Finally, press the hem nice and flat.

CIRCULAR AND CURVED HEMS

For circular and curved hems,
you will only be able to make a
narrow hem. If you try turning up
more than 1 cm (½ in), you will
find that it won't sit flat and will
start to pleat in places.

SEWING A HEM BY MACHINE

1 Set your machine to straight stitch with a stitch length of about 2.5.

2 If your machine has the option of putting the needle to the far left, then do this. This is usually an option on the stitch width dial or it may be a separate stitch altogether – refer to your manual.

3 Line up the inside fold of the turn-up for the hem with the left edge of the presser foot.

4 Start at a side seam. You don't need to reverse because you will go all the way around the hem and finish where you started and then overlap and reverse at the end.

5 Take the pins out as you get to them.

6 Finally press the hem all the way round so it is nice and flat.

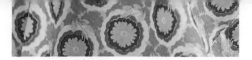

LENGTHEN THE HEM OF A SKIRT OR DRESS

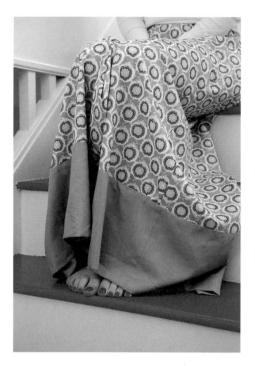

Since I have described how to shorten a garment (see page 80), I couldn't discriminate by not including how to lengthen one too! Sometimes you can add enough length by just unpicking the existing hem and re-stitching with a smaller seam allowance. If not, then adding a contrasting band will both lengthen your skirt or dress and add a new feature.

This idea works best with A-line or full skirts and dresses. When deciding on the fabric to use, try to match the weight of the fabric of the existing garment, and if this isn't possible, make it a lighter rather than heavier fabric. You won't need much so you may be able to use leftover fabric from another project.

YOU WILL NEED
Fabric (for amount, see Steps 1 and 2)
Ruler
Tailor's chalk
Scissors
Tape measure
Pins
Thread
Sewing machine

1   Decide on the additional length you want to add. Then double this and add 2 cm (¾ in) for the seam allowance. This is the width of the fabric you will cut out.

2   The length of the fabric is determined by the existing hem. Measure all the way round the hem and add 2 cm (¾ in) for the seam allowance.

3   Using the ruler and tailor's chalk, mark out the band on the fabric. If there is a selvedge (see page 110), then use this as a guideline for one of the edges. If you don't have a selvedge, then rip the fabric, it will usually rip along the grain and give you a straight edge as a guideline.

4   Unpick the stitching in the existing hem and press it flat. The old hem fold line is where you will stitch on the band, so to make things easy, trim the seam allowance to 1 cm (½ in) so it will match up with the band seam allowance.

5   Take the band and pin the shorter ends, right sides together. Stitch together with a 1 cm (½ in) seam allowance. Press the seam open.

6   Fold over one of the edges of the band to the wrong side by 1 cm (½ in) and press.

7   Pin the other edge of the band to the skirt, right sides together and matching the edges. Line up the band seam to either the side seam or centre back seam.

8 Stitch with a 1 cm (½ in) seam allowance. Press the seam allowance down towards the band.

9 Turn up the folded edge of the band to the inside of the skirt. Align so that the folded edge is 2 mm (⅛ in) over the stitch line. Use a few pins to hold it in position and press flat.

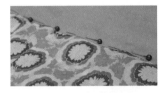

10 Pin from the outside. You will be sewing from this side, so you need to be able to remove the pins easily. Remove the pins from the inside.

11 Set your machine to straight stitch with a stitch length of 2.5 and with the needle in the middle position. With the outside of the skirt facing up, align the centre of the presser foot with the seam between the skirt and the band. The idea is that you 'stitch in the ditch' so that the sewing is barely visible and catches the band edge on the inside. Start sewing at a side seam; you don't need to reverse. When you get back round to where you started, overlap by a few stitches and then reverse.

12 Press the seams and bottom edge.

SHAPE SIDE SEAMS

For dresses or tops that are a little boxy and don't suit being worn with a belt to cinch in the waist, try bringing in the side seams to give them a little more shape. It can make all the difference.

YOU WILL NEED
A friend (!)
Pins
Tape measure
Tailor's chalk
Ruler (optional)
Sewing machine
Thread
Scissors

1 While you are wearing the garment, ask a friend to pin away the excess on both side seams. Remember to make them even. If there is a centre back seam, then you can also take from here. Pin thoroughly, placing pins vertically, parallel to the side seam. The idea is to shape at the waist. You will therefore be taking in most of the fabric at the waist and gradually sloping off above and below.

2 Take off the garment and measure both sides to check that the amounts are even. Re-pin and correct if needed.

3 Starting on one side and with one pin at a time, carefully remove the pins from both layers of fabric – and then put them back in through the top-most layer only. This will mean the pins are marking a line on one side but not holding two layers together. Repeat for the other seam.

4 Turn the garment inside out. Using tailor's chalk, draw a dotted line marking the placement of the pins. You may want to use a ruler to help you keep it smooth. You can then remove the pins from the outside.

5 Before you start stitching it is a good idea to put a few pins back in through both layers of fabric, along the chalk line, so that it doesn't move when you start sewing.

6 Set your machine to straight stitch with a stitch length of 2.5 and with the needle in the middle position. Starting at the top of one side, position the needle so it is in exactly the same spot as the existing stitching. Reverse for two or three stitches and then stitch down the chalk line. Align the centre of the presser foot with the chalk line.

7 When you get to the end, make sure you finish just past the existing stitch line, and reverse stitch.

8 You can either keep the new seam allowance as it is or you can trim it down to 1 cm (½ in) and zigzag the edges or cut with pinking shears to prevent it from fraying.

ELASTICATE THAT WAIST

I have bought a few dresses over the years that have been cute but shapeless. If they are baggy enough and have a waist seam, then one solution is adding elastic to the waist. If you haven't already noticed, I am all for showing off the waist! I think it is the most flattering of looks. This is a quick and easy project.

YOU WILL NEED
5 mm (¼ in) wide elastic (the length depends on the waist of the dress. Measure around the waist's seam and add a little extra just in case)
Thread
Sewing machine
Pins
Scissors

1 Set your machine to zigzag stitch with a stitch length of 2–2.5 and with the width set at 3. The needle will automatically position itself to the left.

2 Turn the dress inside out and fold up the skirt so that you can slide it under the machine and get to the waistline. Starting at a side seam, position the elastic on the waist seam allowance and pin in place. Stitch along the middle of the elastic for a few stitches and reverse so that you have anchored it.

3 Then stretch the elastic with one hand and, with the other hand, keep it positioned on the seam. Continue to stitch along the middle of the stretched elastic all the way round the waist. This is quite fiddly and the further you get round, the more difficult it becomes as the waist starts to gather up. Just go slowly and steadily and stop if you are starting to go off track. To get back on the elastic, lower the needle, lift the presser foot and reposition it.

4 When you get back to the beginning, cut off the remaining elastic and overlap the end of the elastic with the beginning. Reverse stitch to secure the end.

THE PERFECT FIT
Stretch the elastic to suit your needs. Depending on the bagginess of the dress, you can alter how much you stretch the elastic when you are stitching it down. For a looser fit, only stretch it a little, but for a tighter fitting dress, stretch the elastic as much as you can.

ADD BOX PLEATS TO A HEM

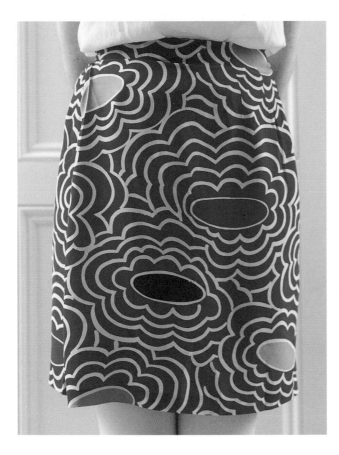

◀ Here is the skirt before I added the pleats. Adding the pleats completely transformed its shape.

Box pleats look fab and are a great way of making a skirt or dress hem narrower. They can turn an A-line skirt into a tulip skirt. They are a little fiddly, so be patient.

I bought this skirt from a vintage shop in East London. I love the fabric but thought the shape was a little boring and so I didn't wear it very much. Box pleats in the hem have made a subtle change to the shape and made it that little bit more funky.

YOU WILL NEED
Skirt or dress that has an A-line shape
Pins
Tape measure
Tailor's chalk
Ruler
Sewing machine
Needle
Thread

1 Decide how many pleats you could fit in the hem. This skirt isn't overly flared so I didn't want to add too many – remember that you still need to be able to walk! I decided on four pleats – two at the front and two at the back.

2 Then decide how big each pleat will be. My front pleats are slightly bigger than the back pleats: 8 cm (3¼ in) at the front and 5 cm (2 in) at the back. You can work this out by folding and pinning them roughly and then try on the skirt to see how it looks and feels.

3 Also decide on where to put the pleats – use a tape measure to make sure they are evenly spread around the hem. Measure from the side seam to what will be the centre of the pleat. Mark the centre with a pin.

4 Divide each pleat measurement in half. So for my 8 cm (3¼ in) pleat I have 4 cm (1¾ in) on one side of the pin and 4 cm (1¾ in) on the other side. Mark these two points with tailor's chalk on the wrong side of the skirt.

5 Now for the tricky bit – match up the two chalk marks, folding the hem so the right sides are together. Pin in place with a second pin. Then, taking a ruler, draw a 5 cm (2 in) line straight through the chalk points. This will be your stitch guideline.

6 Set your machine to straight stitch with a stitch length of 2.5 and with the needle in the middle position. Machine along the stitch guideline.

7 To finish the box pleats and working from the inside, match up the pin in the centre of each pleat with the stitch line. Press the pleat flat with the iron.

8 To help the pleats sit flat on the hem, topstitch on the outside of the skirt, about 2 mm (⅛ in) from the hem edge. Catch the back of the pleat as you stitch. Alternatively, if you don't like the look of topstitching (like me!), slip stitch the back of the pleat to the front of the skirt.

ADD A BOX PLEAT TO A SLEEVE HEM
You can also put a box pleat in a short sleeve hem to make it sit closer to your arm or to create a puff sleeve shape. See page 105 and then follow Steps 2–8.

CHANGING SLEEVES

◀ This is a vintage dress I bought. I love the design but the sleeves ruined it for me!

One of the common annoying features of vintage dresses are the sleeves. They are more 'costumey' than chic and can make you look like you are dressing up or in a period drama. Here are three ideas for what you can do to improve them.

YOU WILL NEED
Stitch unpicker
Scissors
Pins
Needle
Thread
Sewing machine
Tape measure
5 mm (¼ in) wide elastic (for puff sleeves option)
Safety pin (for puff sleeves option)
Ruler
Tailor's chalk

CHOP THEM OFF

If the sleeves are attached to the main body of the garment at the shoulders in a classic way, you can simply unpick the sleeves to remove them and hem the remaining armhole.

1   Unpick the sleeve. Be careful if using a stitch unpicker as the blade in the middle is very sharp. Take it slowly as you don't want to rip your dress!

2   Remove all the unwanted threads from the armhole. If the seam has not been overlocked or finished properly, you will need to add zigzag stitch along the edge to prevent it from fraying. Make sure the zigzag stitching wraps around the edge of the fabric. If you remove the arm of your machine, you will find it easier as you can then slot the armhole of the garment onto the machine.

3   Using the old stitch line as a guide, press under the seam allowance around the armhole. Carefully pin in place all the way round making sure the pins are facing you.

4   Set your machine to straight stitch with a stitch length of 2.5 and with the needle in the middle position. Turn the garment inside out and work from the wrong side so you can see where you need to sew. Start at the underarm/side seam and stitch all the way around the armhole. It is unlikely that the hem will be wider than 1 cm (½ in), so stitch no more than 7 mm (⅜ in) from the edge.

PLEAT THEM

If the sleeves are simply too voluminous, you can take out some of the excess by pleating them.

1 Decide how much you want to take out of each sleeve. This will be the size of the pleat.

2 Iron the sleeves flat, with the underarm seam on the edge. Be sure to press the opposite side of the sleeves, creating an obvious fold line. This will be the starting point for the pleat on each sleeve.

3 Flatten the sleeves so the fold line on each one is sitting on top of the underarm seam. Place a pin in the fold line.

4 The pin marks the centre of the pleat. Now, following the instructions for the 'Add box pleats to a hem' project (see pages 98–101), add a pleat to the hem of each sleeve. For this sleeve I chose to stitch up from the hem for only about 5 mm (¼ in) for a subtle pleat.

PUFF THEM UP

If there is enough volume in the sleeves, you can turn them into puff sleeves. These look more contemporary if the sleeve is short. So if they need shortening, first follow the steps for how to turn up a hem on pages 80–4. This idea works best with sleeves that have a hem to use as a casing.

1   If there isn't a hem to use as a casing, you will need to create one. Fold over 5 mm (¼ in) of the bottom edge of the sleeve to the wrong side and press. Then fold over a further 1 cm (½ in) and press. Pop in some pins to hold the hem in place. Following steps 1–6 of 'Sewing a hem by machine' (see pages 80–4), stitch closed but leave a 1.5 cm (⅝ in) gap by the underarm sleeve.

2   If there is already a hem, unpick 1.5 cm (⅝ in) by the underarm seam so it isn't visible.

3   To work out how much elastic you need, wrap it around your arm. It should be comfortable but tight enough to sit snugly against your arm. Cut the elastic allowing an extra 2 cm (¾ in) for the overlap to join the two ends.

4   Attach a safety pin to one end of the elastic and push the safety pin through the hem to thread through the elastic. Make sure you don't let go of the end!

5   Then overlap the two ends by 1 cm (½ in) and stitch together. An overstitch would do it – the main thing is that it holds firmly, so use a double thread. It doesn't need to be neat as it won't be seen.

6   Stitch the hem back closed again, either with a sewing machine or with a backstitch. Distribute the fullness of the sleeve evenly so that it gathers up.

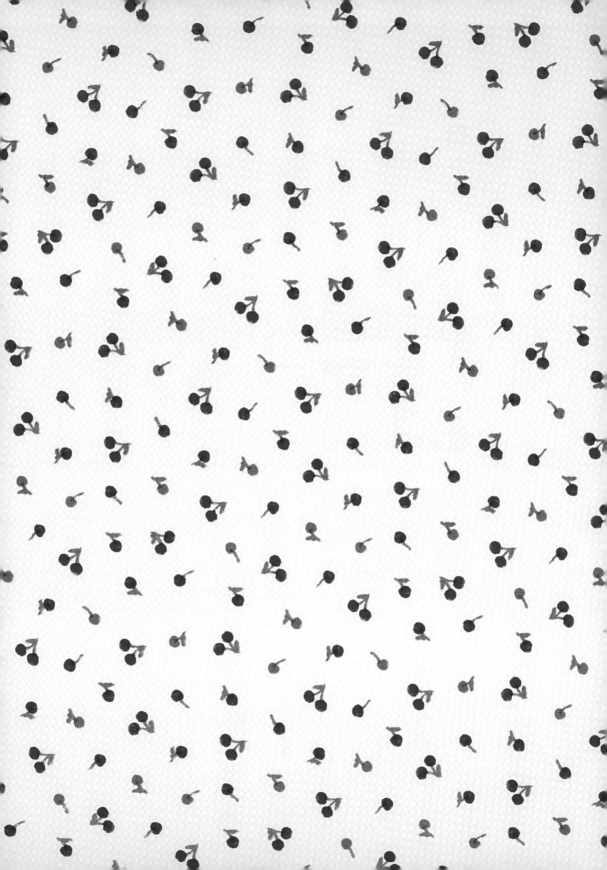

MAKING
ACCESSORIES

CHOOSING YOUR MATERIAL

For most of the projects in this chapter I used fabrics from vintage scarves, cut-offs from hems of dresses and even old tablecloths. But if you don't have anything suitable, then lightweight cotton will suit most projects. Here are a few tips about fabric:

✂ Note the width of the fabric you are buying as this will affect the price and maybe the quantity you will need.

✂ Feel the fabric. Unroll a metre and see how it drapes and falls, this will help you judge whether it's suitable for your project or not.

✂ All fabric bought on a roll or board has a selvedge at either side. It is the stable edge of the fabric and is used as a guideline for the grain of the fabric.

✂ The grain of the fabric is the thread that runs down the fabric, parallel with the selvedge. It is also referred to as the warp.

✂ If you are new to sewing, stick to lightweight woven fabrics such as cotton. Anything stretchy or silky is much harder to sew.

FABRIC EARRINGS

I am addicted to these and am forever making a pair to match my outfit! They are simple yet chic and, depending on the size you make them, they can be statement jewellery or discreet.

YOU WILL NEED
2 self-covering buttons
Pliers
Fabric
Pencil
Scissors
Needle
Thread
Super Glue
2 earring studs
2 butterfly backs

1 Remove the metal loop in each front button piece by pinching it together with pliers.

2 Follow Steps 2–6 of 'Make self-covered buttons' on pages 38–9.

3 Put a couple of small drops of Super Glue onto each earring stud and then place on the flat back of the button. Hold, following the manufacturer's instructions, and leave to dry.

VINTAGE SCARF BELT

This is a great little number for making a T-shirt/jeans combo more interesting. It is one of the easiest and quickest projects in the book, but you will need to make friends with your cobbler.

YOU WILL NEED
A leather belt, old or new (at least 4cm/1.5in wide)
A vintage silk scarf or a strip of fabric
Needle
Thread
Pins
Sewing machine

OTHER FABRICS
If you don't have a vintage scarf, then use any other double-sided silky fabric. Or why not plait fabric for a different take on the idea?

1. Take the belt to your cobbler and ask him or her to remove the middle section – leaving you with the buckle end and the fastening end with holes. Also ask your cobbler to cut out a hole in each piece about 2 cm (¾ in) in diameter, and approximately 1.5 cm (⅝ in) from the ends.

2. Fold the vintage scarf in half across the diagonal. Starting at the long edge, roll it over and over so that you end up with a tube. Pin the last corner down to the rest of the scarf.

3. Take a needle and double thread and make a few little backstitches to anchor the corner down to the rest of the tube.

4. Thread either end of the scarf through the holes in the buckle and fastening pieces of the belt, from front to back so that the end is hidden by the scarf. Pin in place.

5. Try the belt on for size, doing up the buckle. Adjust the scarf so that it fits and functions like the original belt. Then move the pins as necessary at either side to hold the scarf in place.

6. Remove the belt, taking care not to pull out the pins, and tack the scarf ends securely. You can now remove the pins.

7. Using your sewing machine, stitch the ends together using straight stitch, permanently fixing the length of the belt. It is very important to reverse stitch at either end as this seam will take a lot of strain.

VINTAGE SCARF NECKLACE

For some reason I always used to buy vintage scarves, never wear them, and then forget about them at the bottom of my drawer. I was put off by a comment a friend once made – he said I looked like I belonged in the cabin crew of a budget airline as I was sporting a little green scarf around my neck. Neglected scarves no more – they are now funky necklaces. They're really simple to make and you can knock one up in an hour. Take the beads from an unwanted necklace or keep an eye out for interesting ones in your local charity shop. You don't have to use a vintage scarf, any lightweight woven fabric will work too.

YOU WILL NEED
Vintage silk scarf or strip of lightweight fabric (for amount, see Steps 1 and 2)
Round beads of the same size (quantity depends on length)
Tape measure
Tailor's chalk
Scissors
Thread
Sewing machine
Pins
Safety pin
Ruler

1 Decide how long your necklace will be, which may be determined by the size of the scarf. As a rough guide you will need a length of scarf that is approximately twice as long as you want the finished necklace to be. Make a note of this measurement. (You can always join two strips together if your scarf is too small.)

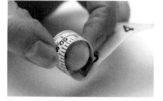

2 Measure the circumference of your beads using a tape measure. This can be quite fiddly, but if in doubt round the figure up rather than down because if you cut the scarf too narrow the beads won't fit. Add 2 cm (¾ in) to this measurement for a seam allowance. This will be the width.

3 Press the scarf and then mark out the measurements from Steps 1 and 2 onto the wrong side using tailor's chalk and a ruler. You may need to join together two or more strips to make the required length. Cut out the strip(s) of fabric.

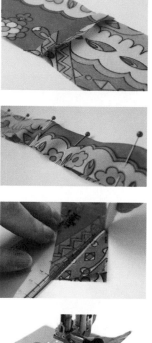

4 If you need to join two pieces to make it longer, place them right sides together and stitch with a 1 cm (½ in) seam allowance, backstitching at the each end. Press the seam open. Trim the seam allowance to 5 mm (¼ in).

5 Fold the strip in half lengthways, placing right sides together and matching up the raw edges. Pop in some pins to hold in place.

6 Using the tailor's chalk and a ruler, at one end of the strip draw a diagonal line from the raw edge to the top point of the folded edge. This will be the stitch line for the end of the necklace.

7 Starting at the end with the chalk line and at the top point, stitch along the line. When you get to the raw edge, stop 1 cm (½ in) in from the edge, put the needle into the fabric, lift up the presser foot and pivot the strip round so that you are now lined up to sew along the strip using a 1 cm (½ in) seam allowance. Sew along the length of the strip and stop about 7 cm (2¾ in) from the end. Remember to make a backstitch at the start and end of the seam.

8 Trim the seam allowance to 3mm (⅛ in) so there is minimal bulk. Turn the strip the right way round – this is a little fiddly and can take a while so be patient.

9 Tie a knot approximately 10–15 cm (4–6 in) from the finished end. Then insert the first bead into the fabric tube, pushing it as close to the knot as possible.

10 Twist the opposite end so the bead is tightly encased, then tie a knot. Push the next bead into the tube, twist and tie a know. Repeat this until you have filled up the necklace as much as you want.

11 At the end tie a final knot leaving the unstitched fabric loose. Using the tailor's chalk and ruler, draw a diagonal line from the open edge to the end of the strip, as you did at the other end.

12 Trim excess fabric to 5 mm (¼ in) from this line (this will be the seam allowance). Fold the excess fabric inside the tie and press flat. Pop some pins in to hold in place and then slip stitch it closed.

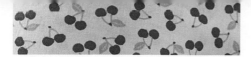

FIFTIES-STYLE HAIRBAND

This is a great little project for using up scraps of fabric. You can knock one up in half an hour.

YOU WILL NEED
Scraps of fabric
Tape measure
Scissors
Pins
Thread
Sewing machine
Tailor's chalk
Ruler

1 Measure, draw and cut a strip of fabric 43 x 15 cm (17 x 6 in). This is for the main band.

2 Measure, draw and cut two strips of fabric each measuring 8 x 30 cm (3¼ x 12 in). These are for the ties.

3 Fold the main band in half lengthways with right sides together and pin. Stitch down the long side with a 1 cm (½ in) seam allowance, reversing for a few stitches at the start and the end. Trim the seam allowance to 5 mm (¼ in).

4 Turn the band the right way round and press flat, positioning the seam in the middle of one side.

5 Take the ties and stitch them together like the band, placing the right sides together.

6 Draw a diagonal line across one end on each tie using a ruler and tailor's chalk. Following this line, stitch from edge to edge. Then trim all seam allowances to 5 mm (¼ in). Repeat for the other tie.

7 Turn the ties the right way round and use a pin to tease the point out. Press with the seam on one edge.

8 At the open end of the ties, tuck in 1 cm (½ in) and press.

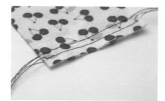

9 Change your machine to the longest stitch length possible. Stitch with a 1 cm (½ in) seam allowance across one end of the band without reversing at the start or end. Don't trim away the loose threads. Then stitch a second time 5 mm (¼ in) nearer the edge, again NOT reversing at the start or end. Repeat at the other end of the band.

10 At one end of the band, pull two of the threads at each side. Use either both of the top threads or both of the lower threads so that the fabric gathers; it won't work if you are pulling the top thread and lower thread at same time.

11 Take the band and insert one of the gathered ends into the open end of one of the ties. Adjust the gathering so the two are a perfect fit. Pin to keep them securely in place.

12 Sew two rows with a straight stitch, one at 2 mm (⅛ in) from the join and the other at 1 cm (1½ in) to make sure it is really secure.

13 Repeat at the other end. You can then tie the band around your head with the ties by the neck or at the front – it's up to you!

CIRCLE CORSAGE

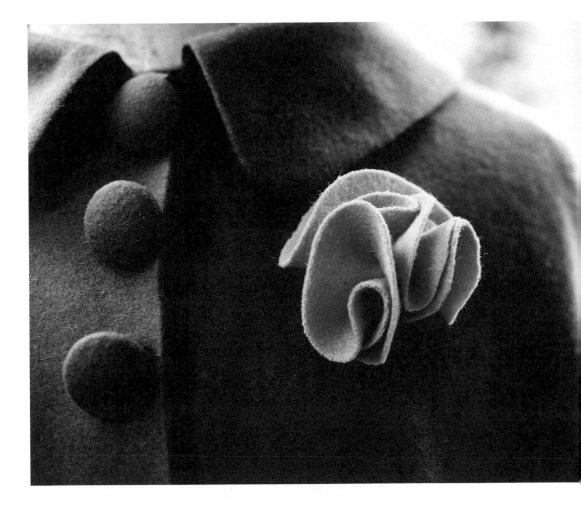

This corsage is simply made with lots of circles of fabric. Choose a fabric that has no obvious difference between the right side and wrong side. You can use anything from wool to tulle, chiffons and cottons. You might also want to experiment with two or three different sizes of circle, which will make it more interesting.

YOU WILL NEED
Cup or something circular
Pencil
Sheet of paper
Fabric
Scissors
Needle
Thread
Safety pin

1 Choose the size of the circles depending on the size of the corsage you want to make. Draw around a glass or cup upturned on a piece of paper to make a template.

2 Cut out all the circles you need. You will need fewer if you are using thick fabric and more for thin fabric. You can also cut out more if you don't have enough to start with, so see how you get on.

3 Take a circle and pinch the middle and twist.

4 Take a needle and double thread. Tie a knot in the end and pass it through the pinch. Repeat with another circle and stitch it to the first one. Continue until you have a full round shape.

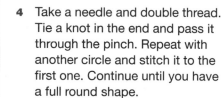

5 Finish by stitching a few times through all the pinches, making sure they are securely attached to one another.

6 Take a safety pin and overstitch plenty of times around the bar to attach it to the fabric circles. *Et voilà* – a corsage!

CORSAGE-TASTIC!
You can make just one corsage as a brooch or hair accessory, or you can make lots and add them to the hem of a skirt or dress.

CUSTOMISE YOUR BAG

Most of us own a basic canvas tote bag. They are really practical but very unglamorous. Armed with some Bondaweb, you can jazz it up in half an hour.

YOU WILL NEED
Bondaweb
Fabric
Self-covering buttons
Scissors
Pins
Needle
Thread
Baking parchment paper
Pencil

1 First you need to find an image. I searched for silhouettes on the internet, but there's nothing to stop you from drawing your own. If your image isn't large enough, you can always enlarge it on a photocopier. Once you have decided on the size, cut around the silhouette.

2 Take the Bondaweb and, following the manufacturer's instructions, iron it on to the back of the fabric that will become your motif. Use the silhouette as a template and draw around the shape onto the Bondaweb and then cut it out. Remember that the image will be reversed when attaching it to the bag.

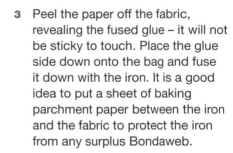

3 Peel the paper off the fabric, revealing the fused glue – it will not be sticky to touch. Place the glue side down onto the bag and fuse it down with the iron. It is a good idea to put a sheet of baking parchment paper between the iron and the fabric to protect the iron from any surplus Bondaweb.

4 Add some fabric-covered buttons in matching fabric (see pages 38–9).

5 You can continue to give your tote a little bit of love by applying most of the ideas in the customising chapter on pages 28–73.

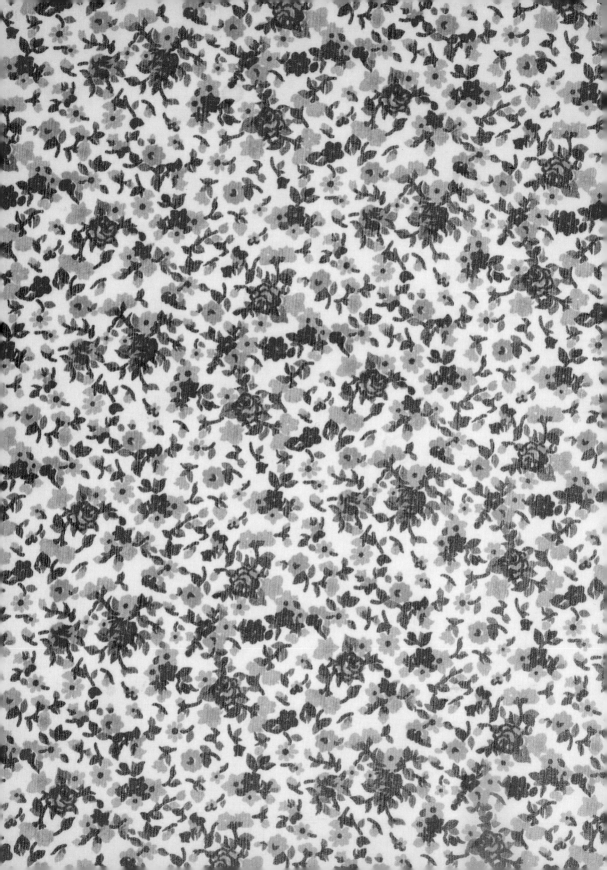

CHALLENGING
YOURSELF

LEARN HOW TO MEASURE YOURSELF

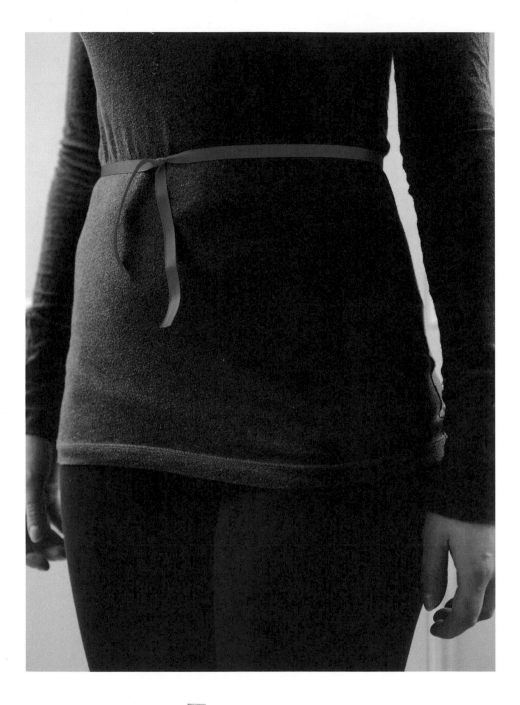

After working in couture where every measurement counts, I have learnt that accurately measuring someone takes real skill. For these projects you only need to take a few measurements, but ask a friend to help. It is also definitely worth measuring yourself in your underwear as you will be surprised how much clothes can add and we don't want that!

✂ Waist: your waist is the soft part above your hip – normally the narrowest part of the torso. Tie a ribbon around your waist first – it will settle in the right place. Then measure around the ribbon. Make sure you are not holding your breath. (I have subconsciously done this before and wondered why my skirt was so tight when it was finished!)

✂ Hip: the hip measurement is the widest point around your hip and over your bottom. This can be at different heights on different people. It is important you measure around your widest point to get an accurate number. Ask a friend to check the tape measure stays level.

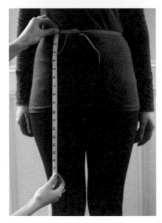

✂ Skirt length: this means from the top of the skirt to the bottom of the hem. You need to be aware of where the skirt is meant to sit – on the waist or below it. Then measure from this point on you. You can keep the ribbon around your waist to help you know where to start from.

MAKE AN ELASTICATED SKIRT FROM SCRATCH

This is the easiest skirt to make as all you need is one piece of fabric. It is best to use lightweight woven fabric such as cotton as the gathering shows up best.

YOU WILL NEED
Tape measure
Woven fabric (for amount,
    see Steps 1 to 3)
Ruler
Tailor's chalk
Set square (optional)
Scissors
Pins
Thread
Sewing machine
Pinking shears
1 large spool of shirring elastic
5 mm (¼ in) wide elastic (the length
    depends on your waist, see Step 11)
Safety pin
Needle

1 Measure around your hips (see page 133) – the skirt must be big enough to fit over your hips with enough room to flare.

2 Add approximately 20 cm (8 in) to your hip measurement for the flare. You will also need an extra 2 cm (¾ in) for seam allowance. For example, the width of fabric you will need could be:
100 cm (39 in) (hip) +
20 cm (8 in) (flare) +
2 cm (¾ in) (seam allowance) =
122 cm (47¾ in).

3 Decide on the length. The design of this skirt is so that it sits on the waist, but you can wear it lower on your hips if you want. Remember to add a 2 cm (¾ in) seam allowance for the top hem and another 2 cm (¾ in) for the bottom hem.

4 Iron the fabric and then draw out your rectangle on the wrong side using the ruler and tailor's chalk. Draw the length of the skirt in line with the selvedge and the width running across the fabric. You may find it useful to use a set square to help you get accurate 90° angles (or you can use the edges of a book). Cut out on the lines.

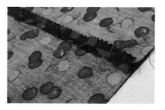

5 Now for some stitching. Place the two shorter edges right sides together and pin in place. Stitch together with a 1 cm (½ in) seam allowance. Trim with pinking shears and press the seam open. This is the centre back seam. You will now have a tube shape.

6 While you are at the ironing board you can prepare the top and bottom hems. For the bottom hem, fold up 1 cm (½ in) to the inside of the skirt. Press. Then fold up another 1 cm (½ in) and press. For the top hem, fold over 5 mm (¼ in) to the inside. Press. Then fold over another 1.5 cm (⅝ in) and press. Pop some pins in to keep the folded edges in place.

7 Stitch down both hems, starting and finishing at the seam. On the top hem leave a 2 cm (¾ in) gap for the 5 mm (¼ in) wide elastic. Reverse stitch at either side of this to prevent the stitches unravelling. Edge stitching looks best, so use a straight stitch to sew 2 mm (⅛ in) from the inner folded edge. Go slowly so that you always catch the edge.

8 Now it's time to use the shirring elastic. Wind the shirring elastic onto the bobbin like you would do with normal thread. You will probably have to do this a few times as this skirt uses a lot. Thread up your sewing machine with the normal sewing thread on top – the elastic only goes in the bobbin underneath.

9 Set your machine to straight stitch with a stitch length of 2.5 and with the needle in the middle position. Starting from the centre back seam of the skirt – approximately 1 cm (½ in) from the stitch line of the top hem – sew as straight as you can using a guide point on the machine. Continue all the way round until you get back to where you started. Make sure your stitch meets and reverse at the start and end as usual.

10 Repeat this for as many lines as you want (I stitched 12 rows), always using the previous line as a guide, lining the edge of the presser foot up against the stitch line so that all the rows are parallel. It gets harder with each line as you have to contend with the elastic doing its magic! Stretch it out as best you can so that the part you are sewing is as flat as possible.

11 To work out how much 5 mm (¼ in) wide elastic you will need, tie it around your waist and stretch it a little, but so it is still comfortable. Cut, allowing an extra 2 cm (¾ in) for the overlap to join the two ends.

12 Attach a safety pin to one end of the elastic and push the safety pin through the hem to thread through the elastic. Make sure you don't let go of the other end.

13 Then overlap the two ends by 1 cm (½ in) and stitch together. An overstitch would do it – the main thing is that it holds firmly, so use a double thread. It doesn't need to be neat as it won't be seen. Hand- or machine stitch the gap in the hem to close it.

A VERY VERSATILE SKIRT

This is another variation on an elasticated skirt. You can use a woven fabric such as cotton, which gives a crisp finish, or crepe or rayon for a more draped, softer look. The finish is best if you use elastic that is at least 4 cm (1¾ in) wide.

YOU WILL NEED

Tape measure
Fabric (for amount, see Steps 1 to 3)
Ruler
Tailor's chalk
Set square (optional)
Scissors
Pins
Thread
Sewing machine
Pinking shears
4 cm (1¾ in) wide (minimum width) elastic (the length depends on your waist, see Step 9)
Safety pin

1   Measure around your hips (see page 133) – the skirt must be big enough to fit over your hips with room to flare.

2   Add approximately 50 cm (20 in) to your hip measurement for the flare. You will also need an extra 2 cm (¾ in) for seam allowance. For example, the width of fabric you will need could be:
100 cm (39 in) (hip) +
50 cm (20 in) (flare) +
2 cm (¾ in) (seam allowance) =
152 cm (59¾ in).

3   Decide on the length. The design of this skirt is so that it sits on the waist. Once you've decided on the length, add a further 1.5 cm (½ in) for seam allowance for the top hem, plus the width of the elastic and 2 cm (¾ in) for the bottom hem.
For example:
50 cm (20 in) (length) +
1.5 cm (⅝ in) (top hem allowance) +
4 cm (1¾ in) (width of elastic) +
2 cm (¾ in) (bottom hem allowance) =
57.5 cm (23 in)

4   Iron the fabric and then draw out your rectangle on the wrong side using the ruler and tailor's chalk. Draw the length of the skirt in line with the selvedge and the width running across the fabric. You may find it useful to use a set square to help you get accurate 90° angles (or you can use the edges of a book). Cut out on the lines.

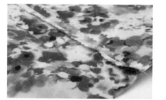

5 Now for some stitching. Place the two shorter edges right sides together and pin in place. Stitch together with a 1 cm (½ in) seam allowance. Trim with pinking shears and press the seam open. This is the centre back seam. You will now have a tube shape.

6 While you are at the ironing board you can prepare the top and bottom hems. For the bottom hem, fold up 1 cm (½ in) to the inside of the skirt. Press. Then fold up another 1 cm (½ in) and press.

7 For the top hem, fold over 1 cm (½ in) of the seam allowance to the inside. Press. Then fold over the remaining allowance (5 mm/¼ in) plus the width of the elastic (4 cm/1¾ in) and press. Pop some pins in to keep the folded edges in place.

8 Stitch down both hems. For the top hem you will need to leave a 4 cm (1¾ in) gap for the elastic, so reverse stitch either side of this to prevent the stitches unravelling. Edge stitching looks best, so use a straight stitch to sew 2 mm (⅛ in) from the inner folded edge. Go slowly so that you always catch the edge.

9 To work out how much elastic you will need, tie it around your waist and stretch it a little, but so it is still comfortable. Cut, allowing an extra 2 cm (¾ in) for the overlap to join the two ends.

10 Attach a safety pin to one end of the elastic and push the safety pin through the hem to thread through the elastic. Make sure you don't let go of the other end.

11 Then overlap the two ends by 1 cm (½ in) and stitch together. An overstitch would do it – the main thing is that it holds firmly, so use a double thread. It doesn't need to be neat as it won't be seen. Hand- or machine stitch the gap in the hem to close it.

PLAITED REVERSIBLE BAG

This is a twist on a tote bag. Straps
are often overlooked when a bag is
designed so I wanted to make them
more interesting. I also like the idea of a
reversible bag as then it goes with twice
as many outfits. You can decide on the
size of bag you want, just measure an
existing bag and add a 1 cm (½ in) seam
allowance on all sides. To make it easier
I have given the measurements of the
bag in the photograph. Any width of
fabric will work for this design.

YOU WILL NEED
2 x 1 m (40 in) length fabric in
    contrasting colours or patterns,
    ideally cotton (based on a fabric
    width of 115 cm)
Thread
Ruler
Tailor's chalk
Set square (optional)
Pins
Scissors
Thread
Sewing machine
Tape measure

1   Iron both pieces of fabric and
    fold each one in half placing the
    selvedges together. Draw a line with
    the ruler and tailor's chalk along the
    selvedge, marking 50 cm (20 in).
    Using a set square (or the edges
    of a book), draw a line at 90° from
    the end of the first line, this time
    measuring 45 cm (18 in). Draw the
    remaining two sides of the rectangle.
    To hold the two layers of fabric
    together, place some pins inside the
    rectangle. Cut along the lines and
    you will have two pieces of fabric.
    Repeat with the contrasting fabric.

2   Take one of the matching pairs of
    fabric, place right sides together
    and stitch along the two long sides
    and one of the shorter sides with
    a 1 cm (½ in) seam allowance. The
    remaining side will be the top of
    the bag so if you are using a fabric
    with an obvious pattern, make sure
    it is facing the right way round.

3   At the corners, stop 1 cm (½ in)
    from the edge of the fabric, lower
    the needle into the fabric, lift the
    presser foot up and pivot the fabric
    around so that you line up with the
    next edge. Drop the presser foot and
    carry on stitching.

4   Cut off the two corners that will be
    the bottom of the bag and press one
    side of the seam allowance open.

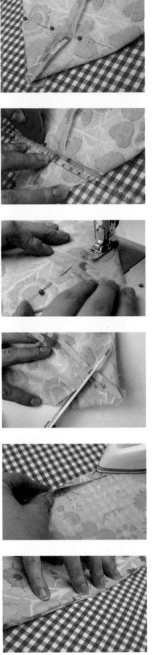

5 Pull the fabric on either side of the bag to align the seams and create a triangle. Pin in place about 6 cm (2½ in) from the point. Repeat for the other corner.

6 Using the ruler and tailor's chalk draw a line from edge to edge, where the pins are.

7 Stitch along this edge, reversing at the start and end to secure the seam.

8 Trim down to a 1 cm (½ in) seam allowance.

9 Press over 1 cm (½ in) all the way around the top of the bag. Then turn the right sides through and press the seams from the outside, ensuring the seam line is at the edge.

10 Repeat Steps 2–9 with the remaining pieces of contrasting fabric.

11 For the strap, make three fabric strips from each fabric (see pages 70–3), each about 3 cm (1¼ in) wide when flat. For shoulder straps they need to be at least 70 cm (28 in) long as plaiting uses more length.

12 Ask a friend to hold the ends of each set of three strips and plait them together. Put a pin in at each end to stop them from unravelling.

13 Drop one bag into the other one, wrong sides together. Put a pin in at 8 cm (3¼ in) from the side seam on each side (four pins in total) to mark the position of the straps. Then pin the top of the bags together, leaving a 2 cm (¾ in) gap at each strap pin.

14 Tuck 2 cm (¾ in) of each plait end between the top of the bags, so they are sandwiched between the layers. Adjust the plaits to your desired length. Pin to hold in place.

15 Stitch around the whole top of the bag 2–3 mm (about ⅛ in) from the edge. When you reach each strap end, reverse stitch back over them to ensure they are securely fastened. Finish by overlapping the stitches where you started.

CARRIE TULLE SKIRT

This skirt was inspired by one that Carrie Bradshaw wears in Sex and the City. It makes a great skirt for parties, although as it's quite sheer you will need to wear it with a little slip. It takes a lot of tulle (a soft net), but it is usually pretty cheap to buy. I have suggested using 6 m (6 yd 20 in), but you can add more if you would like a fuller skirt, or less for something less showy. I have also used two colours of tulle, a pastel green and cream, to make it more interesting.

YOU WILL NEED
Satin (for amount, see Steps 1 to 3)
Tape measure
Ruler
Tailor's chalk
Scissors
Iron-on lightweight interfacing
    (for amount, see Steps 1 to 3)
Pins
6 m (6 yd 20 in) soft tulle (I used
    2 m/2 yd 6 in of cream and
    4 m/4 yd 12 in of green). Most tulle
    has a width of 1.5 m (60 in) but if it
    is narrower, you may need double
    the amount as each piece makes
    two skirt lengths (see Step 7)
Needle
Thread
Sewing machine
5 clear plastic poppers

1   For the waistband, measure around your waist and then add 1 cm (½ in) for a seam allowance at one end and 3 cm (1¼ in) for overlap and seam allowance at the other end. Decide on what width you want your waistband to be and then double that number and add a 2 cm (¾ in) seam allowance.

2   Mark out the measurements onto the back of the satin with the ruler and tailor's chalk, making sure one of the long edges is parallel to (but not incorporating) the selvedge. Cut it out. Use the satin strip as a template to cut out a piece of interfacing piece to exactly the same size.

3   Iron the interfacing, shiny side down (this has the glue), onto the back of the satin strip. This will fuse onto the satin to make it stronger and stiffer.

4   Fold the strip lengthways, wrong sides together, and iron. Then open out and fold 1 cm (½ in) along one of the long edges and press.

5   Lay the tulle on the floor. If you are using two different colours like I did, cut the dominant colour (green) in half, so you have two pieces, each measuring 2 m (2 yd 6 in), plus the 2 m (2 yd 6 in) of cream. If you are using the same colour, then cut into three strips: use a tape measure to mark out the 2 m (2 yd 6 in) points and pop a pin in. Then fold the tulle, aligning the edges and cut along the folds.

6 Decide on what length you would like your skirt to be and add 2 cm (¾ in) for seam allowance.

7 Now for cutting the tulle strips into your chosen skirt length. You should be able to get two skirt lengths out of each 2m (2 yd 6 in) piece. Lay the three pieces of fabric on top of each other and hold in place with weights (I use anything from scissors to tins of food). Measure the skirt length from one selvedge across the width of the tulle using a tape measure. Mark this measurement every 10 cm (4 in) along the entire 2 m (2 yd 6 in) length. Use a ruler to join the dots. Cut along this cutting line.

8 Repeat on the remaining fabric from the opposite selvedge. This will then give you six strips of tulle, each measuring 2 m (2 yd 6 in) long and a width of whatever your skirt length is.

9 Take one piece of tulle and pin the shorter edges together, creating a large tube. Stitch together, starting 15 cm (6 in) in from one end (this will be an opening so that you can get in and out of the skirt). Stitch with a 1 cm (½ in) seam allowance. Repeat with the five other pieces.

10 Now for the gathering the skirt. Take two of the pieces of tulle (of the same colour) and align the top edges. Change your stitch length to the longest possible. Starting at one of the open ends, stitch all the way round the edge, with a 1 cm (½ in) seam allowance. Do not reverse at the start or the end, but leave 10 cm (4 in) of loose thread at each end.

11 To gather, pull on one of the loose threads and push the fabric along. Use either both of the top threads or both of the lower threads; it won't work if you are pulling the top thread and lower thread at same time.

12 Make sure the gathers are evenly dispersed, leaving no 'bald patches'. Use the waistband as a guide and adjust the gathering accordingly. To prevent the gathering from coming undone, put in a pin at each end and wrap the loose threads in a figure of eight around the pins. Repeat Steps 10–12 twice so you end up with three gathered pieces of skirt.

13 Take the waistband and place the unfolded edge right sides together with one of the gathered layers of tulle (for my skirt, this was a green layer).

14 Align the opening of the skirt 1 cm (½ in) from one end of the waistband and 3 cm (1¼ in) at the other end. Adjust the gathering so the skirt fits into the waistband exactly. Pin in place (you can now release the wound thread from the pins).

15 Stitch with just under 1 cm (½ in) seam allowance and with the waistband facing you (rather than the tulle). Be careful that pieces of the tulle skirt don't get caught up in the seam.

16 Repeat Steps 13–15 with each of the remaining two pieces, stitching them over the preceding layers. For my skirt, I sandwiched the cream layer between the two green layers.

17 Fold over the waistband, along the crease line, placing right sides together. Pin and stitch closed at the shorter end (the 1cm/ ½ in end) with a 1 cm (½ in) seam allowance. At the overlap end (the 3cm/1 in end), stitch along the bottom edge, starting where the other stitching finished. When you reach 1 cm (½ in) from the end, turn the fabric through 90° and stitch to the top edge. To turn the fabric, lower your needle into the fabric and lift the presser foot so that you can negotiate the angle. Lower the presser foot again to continue. Trim the seam allowance to neaten. Turn both ends back the right way round.

18 Fold the waistband back along the original crease, pin the pressed edge down, tucking all the seam allowances up under the waistband. Slip stitch in place.

19 Give the waistband a good press. Then stitch two poppers to the overlap of the waistband, one near the top edge and one near the bottom edge. The part of the popper that sticks out goes on the back of the overlap end, and the other part with the hole goes on the other end. Use a needle and double thread and stitch twice through each hole around the edge of the popper, then stitch under and up through to the next hole. Finish with an extra stitch and a magic knot.

20 For the opening in the tulle, you will also need to add three poppers. First fold over 5 mm (¼ in) of the outer two layers of tulle to the wrong side. This will make it stronger for stitching on the poppers. Then stitch one popper 4 cm (1¾ in) from the waistband, one at 8 cm (3¼ in) and the last one at 12 cm (4½ in). Remember to put the poppers the same way round as the waistband.

SIZING YOUR SKIRT

The measurements given for the tulle are based on skirt sizes 8–12. If you wear a size bigger than this, you may want to add up to an extra 50 cm (20 in) per strip. Multiply by three to work out how much extra fabric you need overall. For example, if you are adding 50 cm (20 in), you would need 7.5 m (8 yd 8 in). Alternatively, you can use the same measurements given here and the skirt will not be as densely gathered and therefore less full.

MY FAVOURITE SHOPS

BANG BANG
9 Berwick Street
London W1F 0PJ
020 7494 2042
For amazing one-off vintage pieces.

CLOTH HOUSE
47 & 98 Berwick Street
London
020 7437 5155/020 7287 1555
www.clothhouse.com
An extensive range of fabrics from
cottons and silks to leathers and
really unusual weaves.

FABRICS GALORE
54 Lavender Hill
London SW11 5RH
020 7738 9589
www.fabricsgalore.co.uk
My local fabric shop, stocking a wide
choice of material, all at excellent value.

KLEINS
5 Noel Street
London W1F 8GD
020 7437 6162
www.kleins.co.uk
A treasure chest of haberdashery
and trimmings.

MACCULLOCH AND WALLIS
25-26 Dering Street
London W1S 1AT
020 7629 0311
www.macculloch-wallis.co.uk
Established over a century ago and
selling everything you need, from
fabrics to dressmakers dummies
and haberdashery.

Other cool fabric shops outside
of London:

DITTO FABRICS
21 Kensington Gardens
Brighton BN1 4AL
01273 603 771
www.dittofabrics.co.uk
For unusual and fun
dressmaking material.

DUTTONS FOR BUTTONS
32 Coppergate
York YO1 1NR
01423 502 092
www.duttonsforbuttons.co.uk
The largest selection of buttons
in the UK! I spent many an hour in
here as a child.

BOMBAYSTORES
Bombay Buildings
Shearbridge Road
Bradford BD7 1NX
01274 729993
www.bombaystores.biz
For the magpie in you – amazing
fabrics from all across Asia.

And there is of course **SEW OVER IT** –
we stock fabrics, haberdashery and kits.
78 Landor Road
London SW9 9PH
0207 326 0376
www.sewoverit.co.uk/shop

A special thanks to Fabrics Galore,
McCulloch & Wallis and Bang Bang for
letting us shoot in their beautiful shops.

MY THANKS

As with my sewing cafe *Sew Over It*, there are many people that have made this book happen.

Thank you to Imogen Fortes for giving me this wonderful opportunity. To everyone at Ebury who helped make this book come together, you have all been so lovely to work with. To Laura Herring for her careful editing and wonderful support. To Friederike Huber, for her patience and her great eye for design. To the lovely Tiffany Mumford for her beautiful photos and for making the photo shoot such fun. To Emma Callery for her incredible, fine-tooth-combing copy editing. To the marketing and publicity team at Random House – you guys wowed me from the very beginning.

To my agent Jane Turnbull for coming to the cafe that day and seeing the potential. Thank you for your enthusiasm, encouragement and words of wisdom. To Fanny Blake, for introducing us.

To the girls at Sew Over It, thank you for everything you give. It wouldn't be the same without you.

To my fabulous friends who have put up with a rather 'absent' friend over the past year and have not once complained about it. To my boyfriend, Matt, for his continuous love and support and for putting up with me. To my Mum, who keeps me going and who gave me my work ethic. To my sister, Anna, who always manages to make me laugh. A special thanks to my Dad, for his words, advice and for showing genuine interest in fabric bows, ribbons and sequins.

And, finally, I dedicate this book to Mrs Robinson, without whom, I may never have picked up a needle and thread.

10 9 8 7 6 5 4 3 2 1

Published in 2012 by Ebury Press, an imprint of Ebury Publishing
A Random House Group Company

The Random House Group Limited Reg. No. 954009
Addresses for companies within the Random House Group
can be found at www.randomhouse.co.uk

A CIP catalogue record for this book is available
from the British Library

The Random House Group Limited supports The Forest
Stewardship Council® (FSC®), the leading international forest
certification organisation. Our books carrying the FSC label are
printed on FSC® certified paper. FSC is the only forest
certification scheme endorsed by the leading environmental
organisations, including Greenpeace. Our paper procurement
policy can be found at www.randomhouse.co.uk/environment

To buy books by your favourite authors and register for offers visit
www.randomhouse.co.uk

Printed and bound in China by Toppan Leefung

Design: Friederike Huber
Photography: Tiffany Mumford
Props: Jo Harris

ISBN 9780091947095

MIX
Paper from
responsible sources
FSC
www.fsc.org   FSC® C104723

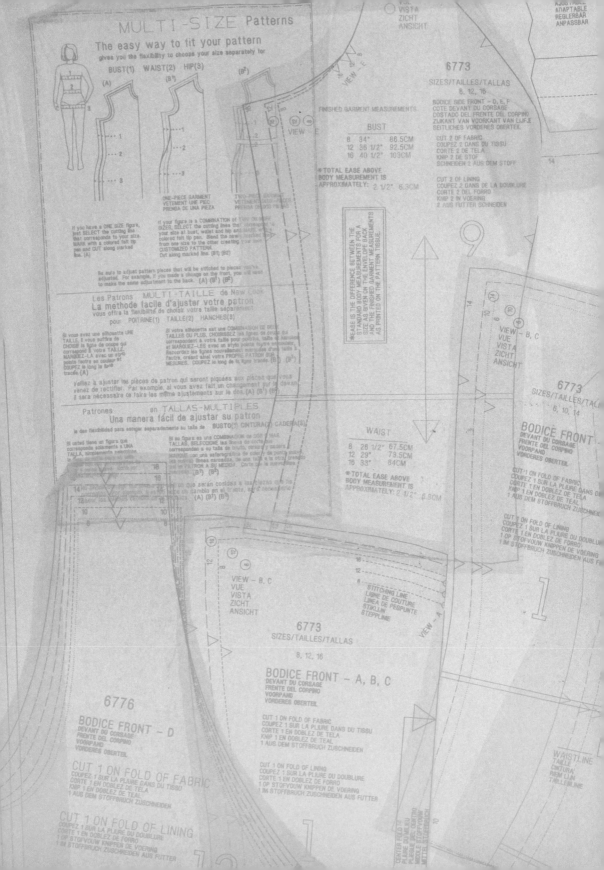